Our Trustworthy God

How Much God Loves You,
Joyfully Engages with You, and
Trusts You
Sarah K. Howley

Our Trustworthy God: How Much God Loves You, Joyfully Engages with You, and Trusts You

Flaming Dove Press
an imprint of
InspiritEncourage LLC
1520 Belle View Blvd #5081
Alexandria, VA 22307
www.inspiritencourage.com

ISBN 978-1-960793-15-7 (e-pub)
ISBN 978-1-960793-13-3 (paperback)
ISBN 978-1-960793-14-0 (large print)

OUR TRUSTWORTHY GOD

Printed in the United States of America

Library of Congress Control Number: 2024925629

Contents

Introduction

"Relationship with God." This phrase appears rather simple. "Relationship" is something we grow up with—family relationships, then schoolmate relationships and those with authority, like teachers. And at some point, we asked Jesus into our hearts to have a relationship with him too.

From that baby-step of acknowledging him as Lord of the universe and of our individual lives, we have the opportunity to grow in intimacy. We have read his Word, we fellowship with others, we pray regularly. We have sought him and created relationship with him.

But in those dark and unwanted circumstances that beset us—grief, loss, upset, disappointment—I struggled to "see" or "feel" that relationship with God who I knew was supposed to be there for me. It is during these difficult times that we hear the phrase, "just trust him! He's got this." But that's not helpful. Trust isn't exactly an on-command kind of reflex. In these moments,

I am more inclined to ask where God *is* than to understand how exactly to trust my unseen God.

When I started a new business and had no qualifications for doing so, I didn't know how to rely on God for his guidance. When my mother was diagnosed with cancer, I didn't know how to accept it was happening and that God was working good things. I wasn't sure how to trust that he was guiding me and that I was hearing him and obeying him. I didn't know if I actually did trust God as a friend or father.

Like a friend we only see at school or work, our relationships with God can sometimes be situational or limiting in how much trust we ever have to put in him. Trust is perhaps something that we all know of and yet find difficult to really define. Is it only relying on someone, to be confident that someone will do what they say? Since God isn't physically here, I wasn't sure how to call him up and ask him to come over and help me process life and all these thoughts, plans, and fears. There was a limitation in my understanding of how to interact with him and trust that he was there. I didn't really understand how to rely on him, but maybe I needed to consider what I defined as trust.

This book comes from a new understanding of what trust means in relationship with God— that trust is mutual, like all relationships are. In the struggle to trust during difficulties, I knew I needed to understand a bit more about biblical trust and if (or how) it was different from the standard definition of "relying on someone." For one year, I decided to focus on the word, meaning, and act of trust. I read several books about it, and each one helped me re-envision my relationship with Christ. I had already read about God and sovereignty, his control, and our choices. These new books helped me delve more into what is between us—between me and God—and our relationship.

I didn't just read what others thought about trust and specifically biblical trust. I tore through scriptures trying to find a better understanding of *two-way* relationships with God. We pray and read, we listen to him, we hear from him. But in relationships, there is more than just talking and listening. An intimacy develops as we form relationships with each other. Dependency and reliance grow as we do in our relationship. This was what I was coming to know and wanted to understand in connection with God.

When I used to work in an office, I would meet people, and we'd have coffee or lunch together. Chatting and getting to know each other over a meal was an easy way to see if this was someone that I wanted to develop a relationship with or leave it superficial, an "at work" friend, or just a colleague.

But some people were the ones that I invited to dinner or to my house. They went beyond the surface, and I shared personal issues, not just work issues. I admitted to these friends that I had problems or needed advice, and they did too. We both shared our lives and the significant things that were going on. We listened and even acted on what we heard; we supported each other with a shoulder to cry on or a sympathetic ear to listen. That intimacy developed. We both shared and listened and leaned and heard; we liked each other.

These were mutual relationships. Eventually, even the mess-ups and the vulnerabilities didn't stand in the way of being comfortable with each other. Whatever happened, I knew I was accepted. We both did.

But I admit it hadn't been a mutual relationship with God, not like those relationships with friends. There wasn't the kind of intimacy of a two-way, *mutual* relationship. But it began to happen as I understood more about him and the trust between us. In understanding more about trust, it broke open some kind of imaginary boundary between me and God. I broke through to intimacy with God and a new near-ness. I stopped worrying and started believing in him and his promises. I stopped just "reading" his Word and began understanding who he is.

I began to understand that he was there when I was uncertain and confused about my business and the products. I came to know that he believed in me and that meant that I could do this "boss" thing, and do it well, as he wanted. I looked back and saw that he was there when I was struggling to understand how cancer could be a good thing. I understood how he felt about what was going on in my life and in my thoughts; and he wanted me to understand what was going on with him and what his thoughts were. He and I, we created a mutual relationship.

What is between you and God? We're going to define the foundation of your relationship to-gether and help you live it out. We'll learn what trust is and how it is portrayed in the Bible, and in doing so, will hopefully help you refresh and re-new your walk with God—and him walking with you—in a mutual trusting friendship.

Relationship with God

Relationships don't usually start out with full intimacy and full trust. When I met the man who eventually became my husband, we started by spending time together. We went for coffee or met for a meal and got to know each other. When one of our coffee-and-a-walk dates turned into eight hours of walking and wandering Rome, Italy, we talked about the connection that had been forming. I bet the kids don't say "going steady" anymore—maybe we could just say that we were committed to each other. But that had nothing to do with what I knew about him and everything to do with the connection we had and the choice to carry the relationship onward. We continue to view our relationship that way: a commitment to each other.

Knowledge was not the foundation of that relationship, and it still isn't. Knowledge I have of my husband, or my friends and family, is not what makes a relationship. I know some things about my husband, for example. However, the relationship is not rooted in the factual information I know about him. The relationship is based on the interactions we have, how we care for one another, how we show our love, how we spend time together, and how we create something (maybe that relationship) together. It is about expressing love, trust, and growth together. My marriage and friendships grow or die based on what we are doing together and sharing with one another, not based on the amount I know about them.

Similarly, I can know a lot about God by reading his Word and by fellowshipping with other believers. But he invites us into a loving, personal relationship with him. He is relational in nature. After all, he is a father, a son, and a spirit all at once—three entities relating to each other as one. He is love by nature, not by characteristic.

Love doesn't just describe him; it is what he is. His essence. God has many character traits like us. Ways we can describe him. One is that he is just (loves justice). Another is that he is trustworthy. In all those traits, the root is always love. He is love as much as I am Sarah. The fundamental thing of God is love; not simply that he loves, but that he *is* love and all of him flows from love. He invites us into that love when we come to him.

He loves us and he loved us first. And what a difficult thing to define! N.T. Wright describes it as, "a mode of knowing that affirms the otherness/rightness of the other (person/God); it is engaging with another with joy and delight. Love is engaging ourselves with another to affirm their self."[1]

We can extend this idea of love to include "acting intentionally in relational response, to God and others, to promote their overall well-being."[2]

So, "God loves" means he affirms who we are, engages with us in joy, and actively pursues our well-being.

He described our interactions throughout the Bible as friend, child, and co-heir, and he sends his Spirit to make a home within us. His love is such that he desires to be with us always as Father, Son, and Holy Spirit. He wants more than knowledge and he enables more than knowledge by loving us first and by the quickening of the Holy Spirit in us.

God also wants more than obedience, which may come from a response to one's authority. Obedience done because of one's authority doesn't strengthen relational intimacy or trust. Obedience to one another based on love and working for another's well-being does strengthen those bonds of intimacy and trust and the connection between two. The relationships that we form encourage mutually working for the other's well-being. God's well-being is promoted by our glorifying him through loving acts to him and our neighbor.

There are many illustrations in the Bible which show us how much God desires more with us, how deeply he wants a relationship with each one of us. One is about an olive tree.

Grafted Olive Tree

Romans 11 explains that we (Gentiles) came from a wild olive tree, whereas the Israelites came from a cultivated olive tree. Our characteristics were different from those of the cultivated tree. The cultivated tree was the one God had set apart from the time of Abraham and made his nation, called his beloved and intended as a light to the nations. We came from a tree which had no such upbringing, no such love, no such intention. Yet, God in his grace and our faith happily grafted us into the cultivated tree.

A wild olive tree expends more energy on the wood parts (branches, trunk, etc.) and less energy on the fruit. This means that the wild olives are smaller, and the olive tree is more of a bush. Cultivated or domesticated olive trees are larger and have thicker flesh on the fruit. The domesticated trees also produce more frequently. So, the tended and cared for trees (or the tended and grafted Gentiles) produce more fruit.

The fruit then is the seed of life. God's love and attention for us is grafted into his cultivated garden, meaning that we too produce more. His caring for our well-being leads to a response of greater life in us. He took something with a different nature and added it within his beloved and called it beloved as well. He shares the nourishment of the trunk with us who were parched; he welcomes us into his Spirit and calls us his own.

Though we were not of the original group, he sought us out and gathered us to himself, bringing us into a new relationship. One where we receive choice sunlight, the best ground for flourishing, already well-established roots, and everything else we need for abundant life.

If a loving relationship is based on acting for the others well-being and engaging with who they are, affirming them—that is what God illustrates with the olive tree. He did not graft the wild olive into an almond, denying our "self." No. He grafted us thereby affirming who we are, engaged with joy by tending the trees, and pursued our well-being to produce fruit in abundance. The tree and the gardener mingle to create something more, something better than what was there before. He sought everything that we would need in order to flourish together with him.

Barriers and Doubts about a Relationship with God

Intimacy with God develops over time as we both understand who the other is and how to depend upon one another. This agricultural illustration for our life in Christ implies the passage of time, the time for the graft to take, and the sap to run through—the time for the trunk and branches to push out new growth that causes them to flourish and bear fruit.

The depth and the *how* of relationships isn't talked about much, at least not in my churches. The grafting, the sap running through, the growth of branches—this depth isn't generally part of the discussion of trusting God. Sometimes I feel as though the Christian world assumes we are born with the knowledge and understanding of how to make healthy relationships, which isn't really the case.

I moved about six months ago and am *still* having difficulty finding people that I can say I have a deepening relationship with. It doesn't come to me naturally, this vulnerability to share about myself and find things in common, to spend time together, and to share experiences. It takes time and more to build a relationship just as the image of the olive tree shows us.

I came to know Jesus as Lord at a young age, but the expectation that I would understand how to have a relationship with him has been fraught with "how do I do this?" moments and long periods of seeking depth and finding little.

Then, to complicate things, he is invisible to us today in a literal sense, unlike for the disciples two thousand years ago, and the relationship with God is one that is a bit lopsided in power. He is the Creator of the universe, the One who set the course of the world in the beginning. I wondered, "How do I approach the invisible Creator of the universe and have a relationship with him?"

In part, I am certain that is why he sent his son, Jesus. He is the one who is approachable since he walked this earth, drew in the dirt, and plucked figs from the trees. He is not so far out there, but rather very much here in time and space. He is more approachable even in the time since his ascension. I can imagine him sitting at a stream together with me when I talk to him in prayer sometimes. Perhaps in *this* place with him I can understand how a relationship with God works.

Mutual Relationship with God

The underlying premise of relationships is that it goes two ways. And in all my years, I had not considered the two-way aspect of our (my) God relationship. Prayer, yes, but talk *and* listen. Two-way *communication*.

Still, even communication is not a relationship. I can communicate with the person at the counter at the grocery store or the department of motor vehicle and even obtain what I need, like groceries or a renewed license. But that communication does not make a relationship. I am not connected to the checkout clerk nor to the transportation employee. It was merely a transactional interaction. It was two-way, but it did not form a personal intimate relationship.

God beckons us into a close, personal, two-way relationship. Jesus did not come to earth to begin transactional relationships with us. He wants every part of us to relate to him: the real and dreamy, the gritty and serious, scary and hilarious—all of it. Sharing all of ourselves takes time. Vulnerability and an intimacy of relationship comes over time, developing varying levels of closeness and emotional connection. We develop the trust that forms the foundation of the relationship.

It's strange though. God knew everything there was to know about me when I started a relationship with him, yet I knew little about him (and likely misunderstood more!). We were not close because even knowing about each other is not a relationship. Knowing can remain in my head and never move toward an emotional connection. That emotional connection comes through more than mere communication and knowledge.

Relationship with God is not just adoration, either. That is what may come *from* my knowing about him, but it could stay on a mental level without moving to personal and intimate sharing. Adoration alone could actually distance us from God by emphasizing the differences between us.

Relationship comes through vulnerability, sharing, and trusting one another. It comes in God sharing with me and me sharing with him. It comes with him working with me as I work with him. *Alongside* each other. It comes in trusting each other and building on that to do and work together more and more.

A relationship with God is built on love, communication, and working for the benefit of one another.

Love

God is love, and he loved us first. When 1 John 4 says God is love, he means it is his nature or inherently him. Like saying we are human. Love cannot be separated from who God is, and his other characteristics come forth from love. We know that the Father sent his Son, Jesus, because of the love that he has for the world, not any other reason. Jesus came to rejoin us to himself; this reaching outside of himself to reattach us to God was done out of love.

We cannot separate love, as defined above, from God. He affirms his creation and delights in engaging with us, working for our well-being constantly.

He loved us first. He began this world by creating everything that we needed before creating us; he provided for our well-being before placing us on earth. His first loving us helps us then understand love and know love as it pours into us.

Building a relationship means focusing on the choice of love rather than an emotion. God made the choice to send his Son to re-establish a relationship with us. This may have an underlying emotion of love, but the choice to do something for the relationship was just that: a choice. He chooses to love you, and nothing will change that. He affirms who you are and delights in you. His choice is based on that and that alone, not on what we have done or will do.

God's love is without limits; his love for you is without limits. There is no cut-off, no need for a do-over. This relationship is based on his love for you. It cannot be measured; I cannot say the relationship is based on how much he loves you. Nope! Because his love either is or is not. There isn't a way to measure it. It is grand—so great that he sent his Son (as John 3:16 says). But the choice to act in love is not based on how much he loves you, but that he does. He loves you and so he acts for your well-being and affirms who you are. There are no conditions on his love for you.

When we come to Christ, we often come because of his love. And we love him as well. Though the relationship did not start with love on both sides, it often carries forth with love for both parts: We love God, and he loves us. God's love teaches us how it is patient, kind and does not fail. We learn the basics of love and grow in love as we grow our relationship.

Communication

Though we don't receive direct texts and calls from God or, on this side of heaven, have the opportunity to grab literal coffee with Jesus, we are important to God, and he communicates with us through his Word, prayer, and the indwelling Holy Spirit.

The Bible—God's Word—is an incredible resource to communicate with him. It is a collection of different genres of stories gathered together to tell us the story of God and man.

> Renowned New Testament scholar N. T. Wright compared Scripture to a five-act play, full of drama and surprise, wherein the people of God are invited into the story to improvise the unfinished, final act. Our ability to faithfully execute our roles in the drama depends on our willingness to enter the narrative, he said, to see how our own stories intersect with the grander epic of God's redemption of the world. Every page of Scripture serves as an invitation—to wonder, to wrestle, to surrender to the adventure.[3]

Evans reminds us that we are not just reading a book but indeed entering into an adventure, a drama, interacting with God through the stories and history of his first people. This invitation is part of the communication between us and God, not merely receiving it (reading), but using it as a springboard of searching and struggling to understand.

The second part of the communication between us is through prayer. If the Bible is how God communicates in writing, prayer is how we most often communicate with God. We have the opportunity to listen to him and hear how he responds, which may be with Bible passages, interactions with the Holy Spirit, words spoken from a loved one, a song, or a million other ways.

We may think that prayer is redundant since God already knows what we want, need, and think (he is omniscient). But I think of it like a child who goes to the park accompanied by her parents. Holding hands the whole way home, the child recounts what happened at the park, even though her dad was there the whole time and saw all of it. Does that make Dad less interested in hearing it? Not at all. The sharing of what happened and what was going on inside her head and body is all the more thrilling because of the importance it shares in the relationship and the unique perspective of the experience. Our sharing opens up the deeper places of relationship. Our sharing opens up the vulnerable places of ourselves to God and deepens the ties between us.

Prayer and the adventure of the Word offer us the deeper, non-transactional ways of developing relationship with God. The other way that includes communication is through the Holy Spirit.

The Holy Spirit is one of the three-persons of God quite literally living inside us. We host another. It sounds like a science-fiction film with a foreign being tucked inside. But instead of thinking of a parasite, we need to think of mutualism, a symbiotic relationship where the species both benefit from their interactions. For example, the relationship between coral and algae is such a mutual relationship. The coral offers a home and nutrients for the algae that grow on them, while the algae produce a sugar that the coral feed on. Both benefit from the relationship.

The Holy Spirit is living inside us, enabling us, and guiding us in his ways, offering the nutrients for us to thrive (like the coral offers the algae). That thriving life comes through the various ways that the Spirit interacts with us:

- Developing our character

- Whispering to our inner self the way to take

- Encouraging us

- Giving us power over sin

- Gifting us with ways to build up the church and others

- Teaching us and opening understanding of the Word

The Spirit is the living God who dwells in us and constantly interacts with us in all our moments. When we wrestle, we wrestle with the Spirit offering the knowledge necessary to continue in our questioning and to reach an end to the struggle. The Spirit guides us in our ways; at times we "sense" that we should do one thing over another, and at other times, we "feel" that the Lord says or nudges us in a direction. "Sensing" or "feeling" from God may be an internal alarm or knowledge that one choice or word is better than another; this is the Holy Spirit speaking to us in our daily life.

And just like I pick back up that southern drawl and certain mannerisms when I return to my hometown and stay with family, we pick up God's mannerisms and ways of speech because of the time spent with the Spirit dwelling in us. The more we listen to his still, small voice, the more we grow spiritually in the likeness of Christ, bearing the fruit of his life in us. That fruit is part of the mutual benefit between us, showing off God in his glory. Sharing ideas and coming to know one another is part of developing a healthy relationship with God. Then we need to act.

Acting for One Another

Relationships formed in love and filled with communication would remain stagnant without acting for the benefit of each other. When I was last involved in a large women's ministry, there were women in the group that I saw once per month, and I loved them. I enjoyed spending time with them in small groups, discussing the topic for the session. But I did not develop the relationship by spending time together to act for their benefit. I had relationships that were somewhere between superficial and healthy. They lacked any kind of depth or intimacy. We are finite beings and have more superficial relationships than deep ones. God, however, is not limited in his being and can have deep, two-way relationships with each one of us.

Spending deliberate time with one another to benefit each other and even form common goals are the pieces that move a superficial relationship to a healthy and growing one. In a relationship with God, this might include fellowship, projects that we work together with him to carry out, or even a project that involves our own growth. This is the time we spend with God in prayer, reading, studying and seeking his Word, sitting in stillness with him. It is also the time that we work, spend time with others, and carry out the plans that we made with God.

Fellowship with other believers provides inter-actions with those whose indwelling presence reveals more of God to us. Each individual is a manifestation of God's creativity and how his Spirit works in and through them. These encoun-ters allow for a new understanding and new type of interaction with God. His other earthly hands and feet show us other ways that he carries out his mission of love for others.

We know or are told that all we do is for the glory of God, but what is great is that we don't do anything alone. With the indwelling Spirit, we together live and work and play. These actions are all in some way related to living out who he created us to be and do. The desires we have to work with figures, tend others, teach others, keep things clean and tidy—all of these kinds of "work" things, along with all kinds of leisure activities like working out and reading, are pro-jects or activities that we do with him to further his aims on earth. Acknowledging him in every activity of our day helps us understand who he is, as well as who we are in him. This deepens the relationship that we are forming.

Thirdly, we have personal projects that God encourages us toward for our own growth. These may involve the classic Christian values and beliefs of forgiveness, expressing emotions in healthy ways, and developing kindness. There are too many to share, but each one is personalized as God approaches you in what you need to live in the freedom that he declares for each of his followers.

These activities all seem to be for our benefit. But they are also for his. He is glorified as we meet with one another and encourage each other. Similarly, he is glorified as we carry out our everyday work and leisure. He is glorified as each of us grows in freedom and stature of Christ. We make him known as we live and move together with him.

These projects, for ourselves or others, are when trust develops in our relationship with God. Working together and needing to believe what the other says and does is what forms the basis of that relationship action. Without trust, we find that our actions may come from a place of obedience or even fear. Trust, though, is a firm foundation for action.

Knowing about God is only the start of relationship with God. Knowing about him is like looking at a staircase but not taking a step to go up the stairs and see what more we may find. Taking each step is likened to the vulnerability and honesty of interactions. Coming to the first landing comes through a deepened understanding of his love for us. As communication opens and vulnerability and honesty become second nature with God, we find ourselves easily working for mutual benefit for each other.

Relationship with God isn't something that I have often heard discussed in church. However, we can learn from him and move into intimacy with him. It is a learnable and doable "skill." God seeks a relationship with us and provides various tools to create that relationship intimately, mutually. When God came down to the Garden of Eden in the evening (Genesis 3:8), Adam and Eve knew the sound of his steps. He has drawn near so that we may also draw near, knowing the sound of our footsteps, the accent in our voice, all of us. With love being the affirming of another and working toward the good of the other, we can see that God has loved us from the beginning of this relationship.

Foundations of Relationship

Intimacy with God, or relationship with him, seems to be a given based on the language we use in Christian circles. We call him "Father" in prayer, and we claim Jesus as our brother. We share a dwelling with the Holy Spirit (hey, roomie!). The depth of these relationships is what we are here to look at, however. Our God is a personal God, a relational God. He is drawn to us as we are drawn to him. But relationships develop over time. Let us consider Abraham as an example of how God builds relationships with us over time.

We are introduced to Abram in Genesis 11, through his family line and marriage to Sarai. The lineage shows us that Abram came from the line of Shem, son of Noah (the one of boat and flood fame). The story then picked back up, telling us that Terah, Abram's father, took his family and set out for Canaan. Abram, his wife Sarai, and his nephew Lot accompanied Terah; however, they did not make it as far as Canaan, stopping and settling in Harran instead.

What We (Don't) Know About Abram

This background information is just a draft of a sketch. We know Abram descended from the line of Noah and that his father, at one time, intended to go to Canaan. But he didn't.

The next chapter relates to us that God told Abram to go and become a father of a great nation, and he set out for Canaan. We are told nothing of who Abram was or what he had done to gain favor with God. Perhaps it was that he had done nothing; perhaps he had lived a life dedicated to God. We don't know. We only know that Abram came from the line of Shem, son of Noah. There was nothing told to us that distinguished Abram from other people that God may have chosen. There is nothing telling us why he was chosen and not his brother or father.

Perhaps what this illustrates is that God did more than love first (1 John 4:19). He seems to have trusted first as well. Genesis 12 opens with God promising to Abram to make him the father a great nation and that he will be blessed and be a blessing; Abram has done nothing that we are aware of to warrant such a promise.

We don't know if it was trust that Abram experienced when he decided to set out as God had commanded. It may have been picking back up the intentions of his own father, it may have been that Harran was a terrible place to live. We know only that he got up to go.

When Abram arrived in the land of Canaan, he stopped and made an altar to God. And God repeated his promise of giving this land to his offspring. This seems to be the two of them checking in with each other. Abram stopped when he arrived in the land where God had sent him, and it is as if he said, "Well, now what?"

God repeated his promise. Abram continued through that territory; he walked the land that God said he would give him, but he did not yet possess it. He even stopped and made another altar, calling on God again. That seems like a place that many of us have been, and a place where it gets hard to wait and trust. We call out, not understanding. These altars and the repetition of the promise show us that communication was part of their relationship.

Maybe Abram didn't trust, since his next move was to leave the area when a famine hit; they went to Egypt. Additionally, he told his wife to say she was his sister, encouraging a lie. That doesn't speak trust to me. During their time in Egypt, Abram did not call on the Lord or make an altar, at least the Bible does not say so. This might indicate that distance had formed between God and Abram.

Abram was reminded of the Lord when he returned to the place where he had previously made an altar—a place, just maybe, he never should have left. And at that altar, Abram once again called out to the Lord.

Eventually Lot had to leave since they had grown so large, living together had become unsustainable. And after Lot left to claim his land, God renewed the promise that all that Abram could see would belong to his descendants.

There seemed to be a closeness and a withdrawal in the relationship. As the old adage goes, "Who moved?" Abram did not seek God. God continued to tell Abram the promise that was coming. God never wavered in the promise and the trust he placed in Abram, but Abram did. Perhaps describing Abram as faithless when he left that promised land as a famine hit and when he called his wife his sister in fear of being killed to obtain her is accurate. But God's promise was steadfast.

Again, God renewed the covenant with Abram in a vision, but Abram expressed his doubt by asking, "but Lord, how can I know?" (Genesis 15:8). The doubt seems to have continued despite the affirmation that God gave, because Abram then laid with his wife's slave and got a son. Thirteen years pass before God again affirmed the promise to Abram and christened him with a new name: Abraham, "father of many nations." His wife was also given a new name; from Sarai, her name was made Sarah. This affirmation of God's faithfulness toward the couple came after the doubt and disbelief shown through their actions. Abraham responded by keeping the covenant and circumcised the males in his household. He received visitors who also announced that his wife, Sarah, would have a child within the year. Abraham received external confirmation of the promises of God. Surely now he too would have developed trust in the Lord.

God steadily trusted him, but even after this additional declaration, Abraham traveled again with his family and again told his wife to say she was his sister. Abraham struggled with doing as God would have him do. God trusted Abraham, but the mutual trust did not seem to have developed.

What We Know About Abraham's Story

Through this entire story, the thing that most strikes me is that no matter what Abra(ha)m did, God continually affirmed the mission he had. God held his trust in him. Abraham wavered time and time again: He lied, he left the promised territory, then lied again. He challenged God. And God was steadfast in his belief that Abraham was the one who would become the father of a blessed nation and reign over that land.

God loved and trusted Abraham, who was not steadfast. So, God needed to verify Abraham's trust. You may know the account that came at this point with Abraham: God asked Abraham to sacrifice his own son, Isaac (Genesis 22). He set out the very next day and went up the hill with only sticks for a sacrificial fire. Finally, Abraham did something that showed he would do anything for God.

The altars that Abraham set up indicate a love of God, an adoration, as well as communication with God. It was at the mention of the altars that we learn Abraham called out to God. What was apparently missing until this point was the common goal, working together for mutual benefit. Abraham seemed to finally set aside his own desires and worked together to achieve what God asked. Though that meant losing his own son. Following this encounter, we do not see Abraham waver again. This was a turning point for the relationship.

That God loved first and trusted first is seen in the account of Abraham's life. It helps me see how much God has loved and trusted me, and still loves and trusts me. It is a reassurance that his love is steadfast and sure despite what I may do. The strength of the relationship, my strength, is the Lord.

Just as God trusted Abraham, he trusts me and you with various things as well—those projects to work on together mentioned before. Abraham was entrusted with founding a nation (one child at a time), and God believed in him the whole time. Every step of the way, God was there. I almost feel like I could hear God cheering Abraham on as he went. It is as though every time God repeated the promise, he was saying, "I trust you; let's do it together."

As a child, I first learned to cook side-by-side with my mom. She didn't hand me a recipe and say to prepare dinner. She knew I could do it (trusted me) but walked with me through it. God too knew Abraham could do it, but walked with him for years before the first steps toward a nation were taken. Trust is what Abraham had to develop before the relationship could move toward a mutual goal. He had to develop trust in God, and apparently did over time.

God knew Abraham so intimately that his actions and reactions were not a surprise. But the relationship needed the affirmation of who Abraham was and who God was. This relationship needed to build the trust factor. A big thing was on the line (the Israelite nation), so the relationship required big trust. Until this point, God had entrusted many things to Abraham, but here we finally see that Abraham also trusted God to deliver on his promises. Perhaps it was the relentless way that God brought him through difficulties or the way that he brought him and his family through harrowing situations. Abraham stepped up and trusted. The relationship seems to have solidified through this encounter, as we are not told of any other occasions where Abraham went his own way as he had before.

Entrusted with the Gospel

It has always been very nerve-wracking to do one of those "trust falls" in a group development or team-building activity. The situation where you stand on a platform about shoulder height above the ground and the group stands behind you, ready to catch you as you fall off the platform. You can't see the people who are going to catch you; they don't know when you will drop back. There is the choice I had to make to trust that they would catch me.

I'm amazed that God made that choice with Abraham—to drop his plans into the hands of a man who didn't always do what God wanted. But he didn't wait to see if Abraham was going to catch the plans. He made the choice to trust and then followed through. What I see in this account of Abraham is evidence that God trusts me (and you!), too. First Thessalonians 2:4 offers more insight into God's trust of us. This verse says,

On the contrary, we speak as those approved by God to be entrusted with the gospel. We are not trying to please people but God, who tests our hearts.

This word "entrusted" jumps off the page at me. Just as God entrusted Abraham with his plans, he has also entrusted us with his plans. To be *entrusted* with the gospel, it says. The word "gospel" is often distilled down to the birth, life, death, and resurrection of Christ to absolve us from our sins. But objectively I have to ask why we care about this absolution of sins. It doesn't get to the underlying point, the reason that death and resurrection are important to us.

Christ came and lived and died and rose, what we call "gospel," in order to reunite us with God in relationship. The relationship had been broken and now Christ established the bridge to start that relationship anew with each one of us. So, *to be "entrusted with the gospel" as this verse says, is to be trusted by God, or invited into relationship with him.* That relationship has natural outpourings that impact our lives and those around us.

Living out this relationship and living with those outpourings means that we change and grow through the Spirit, and we share our relationship with others. Just like when I started dating my husband, I began to share this unique person with my friends and family as the relationship deepened, as trust and love grew. We tell people about those we care about and are important to us. It is the same with our relationship with God; as the relationship and trust grow, so does the opportunity to share about this amazing person in my life! This is usually shared or described as "Christ in me" or "walking with Christ."

This phrase "entrusted with the gospel" sits in the midst of a letter written to believers who needed encouragement. So, this was not just about the relationship with Christ, but also the trust that God already had in them. Confusingly, it says, "we speak as those approved by God to be entrusted with the gospel." I know I cannot earn the approval of God, so what does "approval" mean?

It *seems* to say that God approves us and, as a result, gives us the gospel and we work to please God who tests us. I have learned that I can't earn God's approval by works. He and I are in relationship only by my faith and his love. So, we need to dig a bit deeper into this verse and this approval.

The word "approved" in the original Greek means "to test in order to show that something is acceptable, or to test to reveal what is good or genuine." This word is not used to disprove or show when something is bad and will surely fail. "Approve" conveys the idea that God sees what is good and what we are capable of, and he affirms us. There is no earning of the approval, but a verification of the state of things.[4]

Consider when (or if) a tooth begins to hurt and our gums swell. We have an idea that the problem is a cavity. To confirm this understanding, we visit the dentist, who agrees. We already knew what the issue was, but we have an external affirmation of the current status. Similarly, we have been formed into the person we are, and that is good. God looks upon us and affirms the person we are and therefore "approves" us.

Now that we understand "approval," we should look at the testing. It seems odd to me that something that is approved needs to be tested. What we find is the same root word in the original text of the verse. The words have the same underlying meaning, approved = tested.

God affirms what is acceptable (me) and reveals what is good (me). It does not show that someone fails or is bad. When I taught elementary school, I most enjoyed giving math tests. I knew if the students had done the homework and asked questions, they would all do well. I knew what they had done in that unit and could see when they were ready. A test was only used to affirm their level of knowledge and show them they were capable. I was just verifying what I already knew about each child. This is the approval and test, similar to what God does with us.

He approves and confirms that he is right in his assessment by testing. We could look at the verse in this way, or with a new "modern" translation:

> We have been affirmed by God and are trusted to walk with him who knows our heart and continuously affirms us through new challenges. (1 Thessalonians 2:4, Sarah's version)

In other words, God says, "I know you and I trust you. I trust you in how you respond to difficulties. And I am certain that you will pass the challenge (test) with flying colors."

The testing that God does is not to tear down or bring out the bad in people. It is a building up and affirming of who we are and what we are capable of. It is a stretching and a challenge that he knows we can do. He knows because we are his people, the ones who lean on him and work with him in collaboration. He wants us to grow and move forward, which is why he helps us with the Holy Spirit.

If we consider Abraham, the request to sacrifice Isaac is one that I used to find difficult to reconcile to my loving God. But with the understanding that God knows and approves of who we are and, in testing us, he affirms the person that we are, this story now makes a bit more sense. God and Abraham were in relationship. Though Abraham had done nothing to earn the trust that God placed in him, God loved him and chose that relationship. Abraham too demonstrates those qualities by handing over his son in the testing.

It is easy to see that God trusted Abraham. It is not as easy to see that Abraham trusted God in the account of sacrificing his son, Isaac. It is only in seeing through a lens of long-term relationship based on love, communication, and mutually beneficial actions that I am able to reconcile my loving God with such an ask. To achieve the goal of establishing a nation, God and Abraham had to be on the same page. God never wavered, but Abraham did. This seemingly absurd ask maybe wasn't so absurd to Abraham. He believed that God would make it right in whatever way it needed to be to have a mutually beneficial outcome. What trust! What relationship!

God took the first step of relationship by being vulnerable in trusting Abraham and in trusting us. The basis of any relationship is that trust and love that form. Love, affirming who the other is and working for their best, is demonstrated through trust. God has shown how he trusts and affirms us, as 1 Thessalonians 2:4 says, I am already approved and affirmed. But it throws down a challenge to me as a follower. Do I approve and affirm God? Is he trustworthy of everything—every promise and every blessing? He has laid the foundation of the relationship and waits for us to join him.

Mutually Trusting Relationship with God

I can't count how many times a sermon has ended with "Trust him...Throw it on the altar. Leave it all at the cross." It is said as if it is instinctual or simple. Yet, the *how* of doing it is not obvious or instinctual most of the time. Trust is one of the foundations, if not *the* foundation, of relationships.

We know that relationships are two-way, but I for one had not considered this beyond communicating in prayer. A two-way, mutual relationship with God was more than prayer or reading the Bible. My relationship with him could be more; it could be a trusting relationship built little by little *together*. He trusts a little, I trust a little. Then a little more and a bit more. Until I come to know that I can trust him, and he trusts me. Until we can both trust each other fully. Yet this is what we saw in the long relationship with Abraham. Over time. One gave a little, the other gave a little, and they developed a relationship embedded in trust.

Trust as Action

If we were playing charades and your word to have the team guess without using words was 'trust,' how would you act it out? The challenge in acting it out is that the action is hardly something that I can do on my own. I could try to act out the trust fall mentioned in the last chapter. But it is hard to catch myself in the demonstration. The action is incomplete without someone else. It isn't like throwing a ball or doing grocery shopping. It isn't a visible action we do on our own.

Trust has been called an emotion or belief, "confidence" or "expectation," even a state of being/state of trusting. It has also been called an action. But perhaps the lived reality is that it is both action and feeling. Trust as action leaves me considering what we "do" when trusting and how that impacts the emotional aspect of trust in the relationship.

I can consider the *results* of such action. I am certain the other person will act in expected ways (I trust them), so my response is an action too. I trust that you will arrive or call when you say, and you do, so I wait expectantly. Trust, therefore, seems to be belief *in action*.

There is also the lack of trust to illustrate the point. I generally withhold action when I do not trust. If I do not trust someone, when I give them cash for lunch, I write everything down to be sure my order is correct, and I get the correct amount of change. I act differently when there is no trust.

I had never considered this kind of gradual building of trust and relational intimacy with God. My relationship with God could be based on action and not just reading his Word (knowledge) and communicating (prayer) with him. He is God in three persons, we are made in his image, yet I had not been treating God as person to interact with in this way. I acted in an obedience, which lacked the understanding that when God called me, not only would he be with me, but he *trusted* me, too. His trust in me changed my perspective on the work that I was doing with him.

It reminds me of purchasing a new chair. Let's say that I hear of a furniture maker and research their history, education, and style of design. I like what I learn (knowledge). I go to visit, ask questions, hear about the shop, and may even buy a chair (communication). I may tell the furniture maker that it is very well made and beautiful!

But if I never sit in it, I don't think I could say that I trust the maker. I can see the craftsmanship, the intricate design on the back of the chair, and I may note the sturdy legs and the contour of the seat. I may even inspect the arms and the back of the chair. But if I do not sit in the chair, if I don't *act* on my words and observations, do I truly trust that the chair is well made?

If I believe that God is trustworthy and faithful, that his Word is true and his promises are fulfilled, but I never take risks with God, then do I truly believe them? Do I truly believe that he will support me? Or perhaps I think it more likely I will sit on that chair, and it will collapse under me, and I'll end up in an embarrassed heap on the floor.

Trust as action looks different for each of us. Moses and God's first interaction with each other is a remarkable scene. A bush was in flames, yet it was not consumed. Moses came near and was told that he was standing on holy ground, and God spoke to him. This is the first time we're told where Moses interacts personally with God. God introduced himself and then shared something that they had in common.

Both had seen the misery of the Israelites and especially the slave drivers and the resultant suffering. God loved his people and did not want them to suffer. Moses witnessed their suffering and had even killed one of the Egyptians (Exodus 2:11-12). Both of them wanted to intervene to stop the suffering.[5] This first recorded interaction, found in Exodus 3, was God establishing common ground with Moses, the start of a trusting relationship.

This is our first glimpse of the understanding that God had of Moses at that point in Moses' life. He understood Moses. He felt Moses' desire to free his people from such oppression—he may have even planted that seed of justice. Yet Moses did not see the commonality they shared, did not see who God was. He did not recognize that God believed in him and trusted in him.

He looked at himself and saw a shepherd, a man who had some sort of speech challenge, one who didn't know the elders of his clan. In short, a man others would not believe.

It was a big job that God was handing Moses, but God was opening his heart, sharing who he was, what he wanted, and that his vision aligned with Moses'. It formed a relationship that went beyond whatever knowledge or communication he may have had previously.[6] He was saying, "We are in this together. I trust you in this; you can trust me, too. When you work with me, I will carry you through."

Like Moses, I did not understand that God trusted me. I know there were things I felt totally incapable of carrying out, and walked away from, that I should have stuck with because God trusted me and that would have made all the difference. I also had difficulty understanding how we had shared interests in the work that I was doing. I didn't see that God does more than just accept me as his child; he chooses to *work with* me and through me in trust to achieve his will.

God trusts me. He believes in me.

God believes in you. He trusts you.

He hasn't thrown you off the deep end or left you up a creek without a paddle. He has seen you, loves you, and wants a deep relationship with you. He trusts you in whatever you are in. When you work with him, he will carry you through. He believes in you.

We see this trust grow in a sticky relationship that unspooled from Exodus to Deuteronomy. As the relationship between Moses and God developed, God says something I hope I get to hear said to me as well: "Of all my house, he is the one I trust," (Numbers 12:7 NLT). God stated explicitly that he trusted Moses. Moses was reliable and trustworthy, as the word also translates from Hebrew. God trusted Moses.

I am certain that my life, and maybe your life too, can be sticky and messy. Like Moses, I've made mistakes that must have pushed God away from trusting me rather than drawn him closer. But the end result, because of the love, fellowship, Spirit, and communication, is that we are drawn together and learn to trust each other. I want this two-way mutual trust and nothing less.

Vulnerability and Risk

I want this mutual trust because he has asked me to run a business that I don't know how to run. He has asked me to teach others, and I am not confident in teaching well. I want this trust because I am called to walk together with him as my family member fights cancer. The lack of confidence to carry out what he has entrusted to me has to do with my lack of confidence in his being there, working beside me to achieve the goals and do it well. He trusted that I would do well what he has given me to do. From running a business to walking through tough circumstances, he trusts that I will do well. The gradual development of trust in him means that I am confident he is with me and working toward those shared goals.

That is what gets me excited. This trust means that mutually we are working for each other, and we are confident in that support. I hope at this point that you are as excited about trusting God as I am. That you know you "should" trust him and maybe even want to trust God. *But.*

But it is hard.

But how do I trust someone I can't see?

But what if he wants something different from what I want?

There are a lot of "buts" that may run through your head. They run through mine, I admit. We have seen the accounts in the Bible that show us how scary it is to trust God completely. Moses faced the ruler of a country who sent an army after him and the people he led (Exodus 14). God told Hagar to return to an abusive situation (Genesis 16). Stephen was stoned to death (Acts 7). The people we read about in the Bible who trusted God did not lead easy lives. Today, we who follow God do not lead easy lives either.

The foundation of these relationships we can read in the Bible started out like ours—relatively thin and flimsy—but grew in thickness, depth, and size as experience with one another increased. Growing in trust, however, also required that they opened themselves to being vulnerable. Building a relationship means that we have to step out and risk in order to know if God is trustworthy.

When we meet someone, we make ourselves vulnerable to rejection by "risking" an invitation to coffee or Bible study. We risk if they show up at all or if they show up on time. We are vulnerable in whatever we may share with the person when we actually sit down for that coffee or lunch. How much can we share of our past, our hurts, our fears, our dreams? We decide, calculating each time we open our mouths to speak or pick up our phones to send a message. Always evaluating, this is the case with most friends and colleagues.

Repeated actions and responses—support and indifference—all play into the foundation of a relationship. How we understand who the person is in front of us, if they are worthy of the risk, depends on it.

Perhaps trust is a constant risk assessment until we reach that point of "Yes, I trust you." Once I hit that point of affirmed trust in someone, I don't think about it again. The risk is zeroed out, non-existent. I find that statement "I trust you" to be powerful. It ranks up there with "I love you" in importance.

Over time, the sense of the risk may lessen, or it may increase. When it increases beyond a certain point, we sometimes step back or keep the relationship superficial. In this case, trust has not built a firm foundation but has remained flimsy or small.

This may not be due to any fault, but rather that relationships are give-and-take. We are not always able to invest the time and energy in developing a new relationship and the same may be said for the other person. It is a choice that each person makes.

God too has risked in order to build a relationship with us.

He began by creating the earth and all that is in it, then handing it over to us to manage and care for. He gave up this earth (pretty big thing) that he created and gave it over for safe keeping to his created beings, Adam and Eve. He invited Adam and Eve into his world and opened up to them, vulnerable to their actions and reactions. We know that they broke his trust. That is what we call "the fall" and the introduction of sin. Sin in breaking God's trust or disobeying him.

Yet he did not stop trusting them but came to their aid. He continued to care for them as they went into the creation beyond the garden he had set aside for them. This is the beginning of what we call the greatest story of all time, and it continues similarly: God works for man's well-being and man messes it up, but God continues to love and love and love. Until man had gotten so far away from relationship that he sent his Son to reconcile us to himself.

God risked over and over again to have relationships with us. He loved and trusted and loved and trusted. He keeps getting right back up to love and trust again.

God has been vulnerable with us from the beginning, risking in order to establish a relationship with us.

If we return to Moses, we see that he was vulnerable and saw the risk of living for God. He was filled with "what-ifs." *What if I am not enough, what if they don't believe me, what if I can't speak well?* God answered each of the what-ifs, affirming that God would do what was necessary to ensure the what-ifs had answers.

Moses showed his shortcomings and fears to God. And God accepted him, "warts and all," as we say. Together they went to on to free the Israelites from slavery. But all of that started with each one being vulnerable.

We can gather all the information in the world about God, but it doesn't increase trust until we accept what we know about him is true and act in trust. At some point, we need to respond or act in trust. At some point, we decide that the risk is acceptable.

God made the first step. He said, "I choose you. I trust you." That lowers the risk in my mind because he reached out first. He is all-in. The question is if I am ready to trust him too.

God is Trustworthy

O ne of the challenges that I have had, and perhaps all of us have at some point, is the struggle of seeing terrible circumstances and trying to understand how to trust God in the midst of them. In the last five years, two close family members have been diagnosed with cancer. And the thought comes to mind is, "How could God do this or permit this evil?" It is hard to see loved ones fighting disease and suffering.

In my struggle to trust, this was one of the things that kept me questioning. I maintained a more cerebral relationship with God because I didn't understand how to trust someone who could permit or plan for these bad things to happen.

What I found as I focused on trust in that year-long time included various ideas about how God's world and suffering interact. They were ideas that God did not send suffering into our lives, nor did he allow it. Ideas that God does not choose suffering for us or send it our way. They are theological ideas that have come more to forefront of discussion over the last twenty to thirty years. Some people call them radical ideas and possibly even unbiblical. But the reason I bring them up is because I cannot talk about a mutual relationship of love and trust that, by definition, works for the benefit of the other, without talking about our suffering and God's part in those difficulties.

While we have seen that God tests and affirms us through difficult circumstances, it is not the only way difficult things come into our lives. For example, I don't believe that God affirms us by giving us diseases, nor car accidents, and other such things. He works all things for our good, but I don't think that God is how or why *all* things come about. We discussed in Chapter Two how God may ask difficult things of us to affirm who we are and build trust in our relationships with him, but trust is not what would come from a loving God purposely doing harm.

What I found is that there are three other ways that difficulty and evil may come into our lives: the evil that was revealed in Genesis 3 continues to impact our world, there are evil forces in the spiritual realm that may act upon earth, and lastly, the choices of humankind. None of these say that God caused or permitted bad things to happen.

God is trustworthy because he is good; he is not the source of evil in our lives.

Genesis 3 Impact

A woman once told me that her small group had been praying for a small island nation that had just been devastated by a natural disaster. The leader of the group prayed a bit for the people, then called upon God to continue to convict the people and destroy them because of their sin. My friend and I were horrified at this, calling to mind God's mercy rather than his punishment. Several in the group continued prayers in the same vein—that of God having sent the hurricane on purpose and praising him for destruction. It is difficult for me to reconcile our good God with one that would destroy or punish people in a natural disaster. Jesus has already paid for the sins of all people. No one need pay again, as these prayers seem to imply. The bill was paid. I find it difficult to believe that my loving God would send destruction like a hurricane when his Son has paid it all.

The "blame" for many of these evils seems to be placed on God, and that would make it difficult to trust him. Trusting someone who sends evil my way would be very difficult. And it would go against all that God is. This conclusion that nature is evil and part of God's plan is confusing to me. According to Genesis, God set the world into motion, but then man messed it up, and it continues to spiral out of control. The world was perfect until Adam and Eve introduced sin into the world, at which time it began to fall apart. Some of the falling apart that sin has caused are natural disasters and sickness.

Cancer is not a punishment from God because of our sins, nor is COVID-19, nor HIV. Sickness and disaster came because of original sin, and we now live in a world that has fallen and is falling apart because of it. This was the first impact of the sin that was introduced in the Garden of Eden. Sometimes calamity is just calamity. It wreaks havoc on everyone indiscriminately.

This falling-apart world may impact a nation through a hurricane. But it may also impact an individual or family personally. Both and either will occur for each one of us through our lives.

We are not insulated from these things simply because we are Christians. We still get the flu and as we age, we slow down and may get arthritis. These are things that God did not create in the beginning. These are things have been ushered in by sin and the consequential physical death. God did not intend for them to be a part of our world, and at the end of time, they will cease. The new

Jerusalem that awaits us will not include these impacts of sin.

So, I do not believe the evil that has stricken my loved ones is God-permitted nor God-ordained. It is the natural occurrence of mutations and changes to man's body through the fall and the introduction of physical death to man's world. These are consequences of disobedience to God, starting way back in Genesis 3, and I no longer find that these kinds of evil are reasons to question trusting God.

Evil Forces in the World

The second impact of the fall of man in Genesis 3 is our eyes were opened to evil in the world. God created the world and gave man authority over it and there was no toiling at that time because the earth produced in abundance. Yet, evil already existed, since the serpent clearly drew from that in his temptation of Adam and Eve. It also existed because our "eyes were opened," showing us something that was already there. The sin that Adam and Eve committed took the authority God had given them over the world and offered it to Satan when they chose to believe the serpent's lies over God. From there, the world began to disintegrate, and Satan has enjoyed his authority over earth since then.

During Jesus' temptation in the desert, Jesus did not dispute that Satan could give him authority over the earth (Matthew 4:8-9). Later in John 14:30, Jesus calls Satan the "ruler of this world." This was the second impact of the first sin: Satan and the angels that chose to side with him were given power over this earth.

Satan has enjoyed this authority such that he is often blamed for the illnesses or the natural disasters or the lies that come upon us. While it is true that he influences this world, only three places in the Bible name him as the cause of strife. The doubt and sin in Eden are not one of them, though perhaps the accuser influenced the serpent. The account of Job's troubles and the story of Satan's fall in Revelation as well as a few references in the Gospels are all the attention he gets in the sixty-six books.

Some question the "authority" given to Satan, yet we see that he acts, together with his fallen armies, against God's intentions. He accuses and lies. He blinds the minds of unbelievers. Paul warns us to be aware of his goings on.

Satan continues to have authority over much of the world, since the world is full of nonbelievers. But it is important to recall that he has limited authority and limited power. Satan is a created being, like angels and humans; he does not have the power of God nor the authority. The devil is the deceiver, a liar. He has come to lie, steal, and destroy with the objective being to gain our lives. He uses temptation to encourage sin. He tries every trick in the book, prowling like a lion for his next meal. He influences those he prowls after through lies, deception and temptation.

Whatever Satan may try to influence, he is not omniscient and not omnipresent. He does not know everything and therefore cannot know all. He also is not present everywhere at once. His armies are apparently one-third of the heavenly beings, but even they are not everywhere at once. He is not as powerful as God; there is no competition.

In Genesis, at the time of the introduction of sin, he was given reign over the earth. The war for our eternity began and through the life, death and resurrection of Christ, we know that the war has been won. Satan has lost and now remains in the desperate place of seeing the loss but trying everything to gain what he can. Jesus has won.

The influence of Satan in this time, following Jesus' ascension, is on winning as much territory as possible before the end of the war. Though he has lost, he still has territory to win: souls. The battle line drawn at the end will have unbelievers on one side and believers on the other, with Satan having continued working to gain more people to his side. And believers will have worked with the Holy Spirit to bring people to Christ.

But he has lost his influence over those in the Spirit. We have been released of anything to accuse us of, all sins forgiven, through the death and resurrection of Jesus. Any lie to the contrary is just that: a lie and we have been given the tools to fight such attacks. The armor of God as Paul described is essential to our staying on our guard against this form of evil.

Satan has influence, but Jesus is the victory.

Humankind's Choices

The last reason that we find challenges in our lives is that people make poor choices. At times, we ourselves made poor choices and we must now live with the consequences. We may have chosen one route over another or one sinful act instead of an obedient one. And those choices have likely made our lives easier or more difficult, depending on each one along the path of our lives.

This is the "bad" and "evil" that populate our lives that makes me sad. It makes me sad because each of us could have chosen differently, yet we chose poorly. God made humanity on the sixth day and said we were "good." So perhaps that seed of good is in each one of us, but the influence of the fall has made it such that many people struggle to make good choices all the time.

The more difficult choices to deal with in my opinion are the ones that were not our own. The choice of the drunk to get behind the wheel and the consequence that loved ones lost their lives. The wife who has an affair. The pastor who steals from the church budget. The choices that a son or daughter makes to become a prodigal. The choice of a colleague to engage in fraud to win clients. People, including Christians, make choices that impact others, sometimes for generations. And those choices make our lives difficult and introduce evil into them.

God influences us toward good, but we also have the opportunity to live out that "good" or not. I have never felt like a marionette with strings pulled from above to do or say one thing versus another. I have felt that still, small voice but always had the option to choose.

The first two reasons for evil have to do with activities out of our control. Jesus has already defeated Satan, and we cannot turn back time to undo the Genesis 3 fall. However, this third reason for bad to come into our lives feels like it is within our control to do something about it.

While it is true that we can change our own minds and make good (or at least better) decisions as we mature in Christ, we cannot significantly influence other's choices. We offer words of wisdom and stories or lessons we ourselves learned when we made our own poor choices. However, our advice or suggestions can only go so far. Just as we can help a child study for an exam, we cannot take the exam for them. We can see the decision coming, but we cannot make the choice on their behalf.

Joseph was surrounded by brothers who made several poor choices that introduced bad, or evil, into his life. In Genesis 37, we are told Joseph was sent out to check on his brothers who were pastoring the sheep. When they saw him coming, they plotted to kill him. One instead wanted to profit from the act and suggested selling him as a slave to a group of travelers. The brothers then dirtied Joseph's clothes and tricked their father into believing Joseph had been killed by a wild animal.

The impact of their choices on Joseph was tremendous; he was made a slave and separated from his family. His father as well grieved the loss of Joseph. The poor choices of others impacted

Joseph, just as the poor choices of those around us also impact us. God took this and brought good from it, but things happened as the brothers' choices directed it.

God does not cause the bad things and bad circumstances brought about by these three reasons. It makes sense to say as well that God does not cause all good things in our lives either. Through his love, he is *working* all things for our good, but given the above, he doesn't orchestrate things down to a T.

All of these things are happening around us and influencing our lives. This above list is all influence for the worse. We pray about all of these evil influences as well, against storms and natural disasters or disease, against the devil, against poor choices, but our prayer isn't always visibly or knowingly effective. I believe that God is always intervening and even "interfering," and that we are called the hands and feet of God. He is a still, small voice that influences people and movements around the world, while entrusting us with the work to carry out for him.

Power in God's Kingdom

Even though God may not have *caused* bad in our lives, it's not uncommon to wonder why he doesn't stop the bad. Each of these thoughts or questions are a bit insidious, getting under our skin and infecting our understanding of who God is and how trustworthy he is. Wondering why God doesn't stop bad things from happening gets at how power works in the kingdom where love reigns. Jesus talks about this Kingdom in Mark 10:42-45:

So Jesus called them together and said, "You know that the rulers in this world lord it over their people, and officials flaunt their authority over those under them. But among you it will be different. Whoever wants to be a leader among you must be your servant, and whoever wants to be first among you must be the slave of everyone else. For even the Son of Man came not to be served but to serve others and to give his life as a ransom for many."

We wonder why God doesn't step in to change the circumstances, alter the choices that we or others have made, stop spirits from influencing the world, or hold back the evil that is wrought upon earth. That kind of power is the lording-it-over-them power. It is not servant power.

We began by defining love as affirming others, engaging with them in joy, and actively pursuing the other's well-being. The thing about defining love this way is that it leaves no room for control. When I began to understand more about the difference between lording power and servant power, I realized that I had confused power with control. I think control is the "lording" power, yet that is what Jesus says is not his way. So, I began to question if God was "in control."

In Genesis 3:16, we are first introduced to the kind of power that was not servant based. After the fall, man was cursed, and part of that curse was for the husband to "rule over" the wife. This "lording-over" power was not the original relationship power but the direct result of disobedience.

But Jesus came to re-establish the Kingdom of God on earth, and he modeled and taught servant power. Jesus served and loved those he interacted with in the Gospel accounts, effectively declaring that "lording" power was not his way.

He came to break the curse of sin, this kind of power being one of those.

When we talk of "lording over" power, or some might call it "control," I imagine a marionette, a child's entertainment. Each move is played out by another person. The doll makes no choices, doesn't even walk on his own.

Another image of control may be of God as a circus tamer, ensuring that we go this way or that with the flick of a wrist, holding a lasso or whip, issuing a threat, or reminding the animal of their training.

These ideas leave no room for personality or individualism in who we are, only the ability to follow/puppet our creator. These ideas leave no room for the God who is love.

Good parenting experts would say a child needs to make their own mistakes and learn from them, while also desiring that the child make good and right choices. But society calls parents who decide for and "control" a child a "helicopter parent," meant to ridicule the situation. We expect that a child with helicopter parenting will grow up unable to contribute to a productive society as they could have if given the opportunity to learn things as they grow. God is the ultimate parent and so works much the same way as "good parenting" would guide us.

Some may call on examples from the Bible. Proverbs 16:9 and 19:21, as well as Job 42:2, all speak of God's purposes in the face of man's plans. I find that God's *purposes* are not the same as his *orders*, controlling my first step and the reaction, second step and consequence, and so on. His purpose may be to teach me patience, generosity, or some other godly trait. Those can be learned in any number of ways, not just one. Based on the decisions that we make, we will find ourselves in situations where that characteristic comes to the forefront of our challenges, for example.

We have Romans 8:28 which tells us this explicitly, "We know that in everything God works for good with those who love him, who are called according to his purpose," (RSV). God, who loves us, works together with us (who love him and work for his purpose), to bring about good in all circumstances. This verse is key in noting that God works *with* those who love him; he cooperates with us, others and creation to bring about the good that he intends. This is how the power of God works; rather than controlling others, it is working with them.

We also find examples that are used to point out that God controls. I can think of Pharoah as Moses called on him to release the Israelites to go and worship God. Seven times, Pharaoh hardened his own heart, and three times God hardened Pharaoh's heart.

At the sixth plague, we are told that God hardened Pharoah's heart. The words that are used in the original Hebrew provide a dual meaning of both hardening the heart and making stubborn or stronger in will. The Message translation says that God "made Pharoah stubborn as ever," in Exodus 10:20. The implication here is that Pharaoh had made his choice and that God gave him the strength of will and heart to maintain his position, or "keep him to his word" and not to change it. In the next plague, we find again that it was Pharaoh who hardened his own heart.

God was not controlling Pharoah in the account of the plagues as the words may seem to say. He recognized who Pharoah was and helped him stand firm in his (Pharoah's) own convictions. It was Pharoah's convictions that led to the hardening in the first place. Hardening of the heart came from disobedience to God, which Pharoah himself identified and called himself out for (Exodus 9:27; 10:16-17). It was Pharoah's sin that hardened his heart, and God saw what was happening and loved Pharoah as his own creation. He knew who Pharaoh was and supported his heart to carry on.[7]

God made it such that the heart of Pharoah would be strong enough to withstand his own decisions. He helped him live the life that he chose to live, with all its good and bad, sorrow and joy. He made his own way though God also gave him ten chances to change his mind (heart). God was not happy to see one of his own creations making these decisions, but he used them for good. Pharoah chose the way of sin instead of righteousness. But God did not control Pharoah or the situation that they were in, nor did he manipulate to gain a certain outcome, though we might say he influenced it. He loved all those involved and worked for their well-being. God asked Pharoah time after time to simply let his people go, but Pharoah refused. God loved Pharaoh and used his power to influence the situation, but did not use "lording-over" power.

Let us consider another example where "seeing" God's wrath is prevalent, yet perhaps I do not see wrath any longer. In Numbers 16, we read of a group of 250 men who grumbled at Moses and came against him. The next day, this group stood together while Moses and Aaron stood together, waiting for God to decide who was right in their assessment. God distinguished (judged) the heart of those who believed from those who did not. Again, we see that people made their own choices about who or what was their god (small g), and their hearts were revealed.

The following day, more people came to grumble against Moses, and God's wrath was stoked. I very much dislike this word—*wrath*—because we associate it with our own faulty, sinful anger and the way we act or react to anger. His wrath comes from a righteous anger. In this case we find that more people came in unbelief. He was angry, having given them everything necessary to live and a place to belong with him. How could these people reject him and his love for them? They made their own choices, and God responded to those choices according to their hearts, not his own.

I can see no place where God has caused or inflicted pain and hardship on people in the Bible. God has, however, responded and discerned the heart of people who sinned.

Biblical References to God's Control

The thoughts that he either controls the world or he allows bad things to happen inside of it embrace the idea that God is in control. But I am no longer so sure that he does. What I have recently come across in understanding how God works has led me to reflect a lot. If he does not use this "lording over it" kind of power then the Bible may say something else.

The following ideas are just that—ideas. They are ideas that I find help me understand better how to trust God in the face of evil, particularly when I consider that God is love, he is faithful, and he is good. I know that not everyone will agree with the theories, but they will certainly give you something to discuss in your small groups and Sunday School classes.

I want to be clear that I'm not a Hebrew or Greek scholar, and those who are will weigh these words differently than I do. I offer what follows not as proof, but because it opened a door for me — a hint that even the names we render "almighty" may carry more tenderness, nourishment, and sustaining than raw force. I share it as an invitation to look again, not a case I'm asking anyone to defend.

There has been considerable study over the words translated "almighty" and "omnipotent" in recent decades, based on even older publications. This research shows that translations are imperfect, though God's Word is solid.

El-Shaddai and Sabaoth are the two Hebrew words/phrases that have been translated as "almighty" in our modern Bibles. The root of the words, however, offer a different picture. El-Shaddai has connotations of fertility, with scholars saying that the meaning in Genesis is closer to "God who blesses or nourishes" (sometimes referred to as "God of breasts") and later in Scripture, referring to a protective God. These passages describe the nourishing and protective qualities of a mother, not the power referring to omnipotence. The idiom that is drawn by the idea of nourishment at the breast of God, as loving mother, gathering her people to herself to sustain at her own breast, is striking in its tenderness. But it is lacking in any idea of omnipotence or control.

Sabaoth first caught my attention when I lived in Italy, as church members would refer to "Il Signore degli Eserciti." The Lord of the Armies is the Italian-English translation, while my Bible merely says "almighty," and the direct translation is "Lord of Hosts." I knew what the words meant but didn't understand the idea behind the name until I came across "God of the Angel Armies" and considered context. The title pictures God surrounded and served by the hosts of heaven — not a lone strongman wielding raw force, but the One around whom all of heaven gathers. Even here, in the most martial of God's names, the image is of God accompanied and served in love, rather than dominating alone. The name that sounds most like brute power, looked at closely, still opens toward relationship.

First Corinthians 13:4-6 explains that love is patient, does not dishonor others, doesn't delight in evil; love protects. Since God is love, these things wrap up to indicate to me that God does not violate others. Love does not violate others; therefore, God could not wrest control from everyone. Our autonomy, or power over ourselves, is precious to our God who is love.

The third and final translation of "almighty" we find is that in the New Testament Greek. The initial translation from Hebrew to Greek was called the Septuagint. This version of the Old Testament documents utilized a word which was apparently coined for use in the translation, *pantokrator*. Better translated, it says "all-holding" or "all-sustaining" when considering the roots of this compound word. There is no reference to power at all in the underlying Greek.

This idea of power was introduced only when a Latin version was made several centuries after

Christ. In the Latin Vulgate, this idea of *pantokrator* is translated *omnipotens*, and we see quickly where the misunderstanding came from (omnipotence or all-power). A translation to Latin from a translation of the Greek didn't maintain the original meaning.

These ideas may feel radical, yet my biggest struggle in thinking that is that languages have rules in their use. Just as I have learned there are multiple words to be used for "happy" when I speak in Italian, there are multiple words we can use in English for Greek and Hebrew translation. The struggle I have is that the nuances that El-Shaddai, Sabaoth, and *pantokrator* have do not seem to come close to all-powerful.

While this lack of omnipotence in the original languages may leave us stunned, it also leaves us with the possibility of God holding an unexpected kind of power. A power that answers the contradiction of "If God is all-powerful (if God is in control), how is there so much evil in the world?" He doesn't hold all power. Because God's nature is love, he cannot violate who a person is by manipulating them into *not* doing the ill they wish to do. He does not violate who we are in order to achieve his purposes; he works with us.

God's Love-Power

God's loving nature drives all of his actions, the affirming who we are and the benefitting the other. Additionally, we know that love is compelled to respect the boundaries of the individual and cannot violate a person. Because of this central aspect of love, God cannot control others, nor can he control the evil in the world. Yet he is the One who works *for* the good of those he created, and never against. God is trustworthy and he is love. He has not planned or sent our way the bad and evil that has come into our lives. He instead is working and active in defeating evil. His Son has already defeated it! He suffered and now experiences the suffering that we walk through not only by his Word, but through the presence of his Spirit.

God's power is in the love that he has for each of us and the influence that love has on our actions and the world around us. His influence in the world grows as our love grows. As he is introduced to more people through missions and simply living our lives in Christ, his influence grows and his power to effect change is then also enlarged. Our cooperation with him and the cooperation of others with him bring about the good that he intends for us. He works good in our lives, and he can take what others intend for evil and make it turn out for good; that is more effective when we work with him.

God is trustworthy. He is faithful to his promises and cooperates to bring about good in our lives. When we are hurt by someone, God would like to change what they said or what they did. But he loves that person as much as he loves us. He does what is good for them and for you. He doesn't violate the person who inflicted the harm on us because his actions are driven by love. He also ensures that vengeance is his. Your pain has been lived and experienced by God himself...on the cross and through the Spirit in you.

God's love works within the fallen world of sin. These two battle constantly, though we know the end result: Jesus already won. To me, Christ's victory strengthens the argument that God is trustworthy; he has gone before us to already defeat the evil. [8]

Some may wonder how a God who does not control can still promise that evil is already defeated. It's a fair question, and I sit with it too. The victory I'm describing isn't God overpowering the world into submission — that would be the very "lording" power Jesus refused. It's that love has already proven, at the cross and the empty tomb, that it outlasts and outloves everything set against it. God's triumph is not the certainty of a puppeteer who controls every outcome, but the certainty of a love that nothing — not death, not evil, not our worst choices — has been able to extinguish, and that keeps working, patiently and relentlessly, toward good. That is a different kind of sure thing. To me it is a deeper one.

This is Love that treasures all of creation such that he desires to give all an opportunity to choose him.

Are You Trustworthy?

G od works for our good, all the time out of his love for us. Through opportunities of working together, we build trust. The Parable of the Talents found in Matthew 25:14-30 shares an interesting perspective of a master who entrusted his servants with gold. (There is that word again, "entrust.") The parable goes something like this.

> Again, it will be like a man going on a journey, who called his servants and entrusted his wealth to them. To one he gave five bags of gold, to another two bags, and to another one bag, each according to his ability. Then he went on his journey. The man who had received five bags of gold went at once and put his money to work and gained five bags more. So also, the one with two bags of gold gained two more. But the man who had received

one bag went off, dug a hole in the ground and hid his master's money.

After a long time the master of those servants returned and settled accounts with them. The man who had received five bags of gold brought the other five. "Master," he said, "you entrusted me with five bags of gold. See, I have gained five more."

His master replied, "Well done, good and faithful servant! You have been faithful with a few things; I will put you in charge of many things. Come and share your master's happiness!"

The man with two bags of gold also came. "Master," he said, "you entrusted me with two bags of gold; see, I have gained two more."

His master replied, "Well done, good and faithful servant! You have been faithful with a few things; I will put you in charge of many things. Come and share your master's happiness!"

Then the man who had received one bag of gold came. "Master," he said, "I knew that you are a hard man, harvesting where you have not sown and gathering where you have not scattered seed. So I was afraid and went out and hid your gold in the ground. See, here is what belongs to you."

His master replied, "You wicked, lazy servant! So you knew that I harvest where I have not sown and gather where I have not scattered seed? Well then, you should have put my money on deposit with the bankers, so that when I returned I would have received it back with interest. So take the bag of gold from him and give it to the one who has ten bags. For whoever has will be given more, and they will have an abundance. Whoever does not have, even what they have will be taken from them. And

throw that worthless servant outside,
into the darkness, where there will be
weeping and gnashing of teeth."

This parable reveals a number of things about what God expects and trusts his servants to do. As an analogy, this parable at its simplest understanding gives us some ideas about how God trusts us and how our cooperation with him works out. The master represents our Lord and master, Jesus. The servants are those who work for and with the master, just as we work for and with Jesus.

The master called his servants. We assume all of his servants, so perhaps there were three. Each servant varied in his or her capabilities and experience, but each could do something according to their ability. The master had worked with them for long enough that a relationship had developed in which they knew each other on some level. The master understood their capabilities and they understood they should do something with the gold.

The parable does not include instructions to go out and plant wheat for a good return. Nor was there instruction to harvest the olive fruit, paying the press to make it into oil and then selling it. The master entrusted the money, his money, to each and left. He allowed the shared objective or project of utilizing the talents to being a return as enough.

I feel this way at times. Lord, you gave me this skill of organizing or leadership, but what do you want me to do with it? He hasn't given me instructions to go to this place or that and assist or lead. He leaves that to each of us according to our ability and interest. He leaves it to us to follow the heart that he gave us.

The bags of money are called "talents" in other versions, and that is much easier to think of in non-monetary ways. For the things that have been entrusted to us may indeed be money but are more often the gifts and talents of character and action.

As the Apostle Paul says in 1 Corinthians 12, each is given by the Spirit different kinds of gifts. Verses 4 and 7 say, "There are different kinds of gifts, but the same Spirit distributes them...Now to each one the manifestation of the Spirit is given for the common good."

Each of us is gifted by the Spirit to carry out the work we do; the Spirit offers talents and giftings to glorify God and love others well. This outpouring of the Spirit allows us to love well, through ordinary and spiritual workings.

God has given us something to work with, each one. From one or five or even ten various talents or treasures. He has entrusted us to work with them and yield for his kingdom. Doing everything as to the Lord (Colossians 3:23).

Despite having been given no direct instruction, both the five-bag servant and two-bag servant doubled the amount the master had given them. The text says they "went at once and put the money to work." It doesn't seem there was any doubt, since they went immediately. They understood their own abilities and perhaps they also were upheld by the trust the master had in them to be able to do something with the treasure.

I find when others support me, especially those with positions of responsibility, it is much easier to believe in myself as well. This is the incredible point about God trusting me. The Creator, the Father of us all, believes that I can, and he walks with me to do his will with these talents. He is not away on the long journey like the master was. He has already returned, sending his Spirit to assist in all we do (Acts 13:4; Ephesians 1:17).

The master's displeasure comes only with the one who tried nothing. The servant didn't even do the bare minimum of earning interest on the coin. This was a difficult part of the passage for me for a long time. Until I understood that the issue was the relationship. While the master understood and trusted that the servant could manage well one bag, the servant did not know the master at all.

The servant called the master "a hard man" and claimed that he reaped what he did not sow. We know this master. He is the same who gave his own life that we may live because he loved us so. I would not describe the Lord as a "hard" person, and I know that his touch is enough for crops or people to flourish in extraordinary ways. I describe him as loving and kind, generous of spirit and hand. I could go on, but I think you see the difference between what the first servants believed about the master and what the last believed.

The wicked servant filled with fear rather than awe. He was afraid and cowered in the face of his master. He did not walk knowing that the master approved of him and believed he was capable. He hid and did nothing. The servant had the opportunity to know the master, working alongside him regularly. Yet he rejected who the master really was and so was cast from his presence because of his *own* decision. The master did not make the decision to throw him out into darkness; the servant made the choice to reject the master.

And the master rightly judged, or assessed, the servant's heart and responded.

So, this parable offers us the opportunity to consider our own actions—our talents and treasure and how they are employed. It invites us to think about the fear that we have of the Lord, if it leaves us cowering or standing in awe.

While it is true that the final servant had his money taken away, and that indicates that we too could see our talents and treasures diminished, there is still hope. Even when I have fallen short, I know that my faithfulness with what has been entrusted to me will open the possibility of more being given to me. God only gives according to ability, and it seems he gave and then with the demonstration that the ability and trust were affirmed, he entrusted them with more, just as we see in the relationship with Abraham and in 1 Thessalonians 2:4.

It makes me wonder what I have done with the gold (time, treasure, talent) that has been entrusted to me. I am certain I have fallen short, but taking time to reflect, I can also see that that shortfall can be shored up and with God's help, regained.

Entrusted and Guided to Fulfill the Gospel

Peter was present at the Great Commission, the co-mission ("Co-" meaning together). This too speaks of cooperating with God. Peter was charged with making disciples of all nations in Matthew 28. And he was present when the Spirit came upon the disciples, as described in Acts 1:8, "But you will receive power when the Holy Spirit comes on you; and you will be my witnesses in Jerusalem, and in all Judea and Samaria, and to the ends of the earth."

In Jerusalem...Judea...Samaria, and the rest of the world.

Research shows that ten years pass before we arrive at Acts 10 and 11. Peter had been spreading the gospel in Jerusalem all those years. The Spirit of God himself was with him, guiding him in this mission entrusted to him (and others), as the verse above states. Yet we see in chapters 10 and 11 that God wants him to move onward, outward. God wanted Peter to move beyond the area of Jerusalem where he was living and preaching. So, he sent a vision to Peter in order to equip him.

Peter had certain ideas about what was appropriate, what was pure and acceptable for a Jew to do. Based on Jewish tradition that associating with Gentiles would make one ritually unclean, Peter did not associate with them. Peter wasn't ready even though God had entrusted him with witnessing to the nations. For ten years, Peter had not done as the commission had instructed.

I have often felt or worried that I am not doing what God would have me do. For example, I've wondered if I am doing enough in the women's ministry or in my writing ministry. I take heart with this story of Peter because he had been called to do something and when it was time for him to do things differently, God sent a message to him.

God equipped him, through a vision which changed his heart and mind, turning him away from man's rules and toward God's instruction. Let me also be honest that I am so glad to see that God didn't give up after the first vision but showed Peter three times what was good in his eyes. This gives me hope that God will also make it clear to me, even using multiple means, to ensure that I carry out what he has entrusted to me.

So, when men from a Gentile household sought out Peter, he was tested. The test was if he would go with these who others may call "unclean," and he did. God affirmed Peter through the visions and approved of him when he went to visit the house of a Gentile. He trusted Peter and sent the Holy Spirit to that Gentile household to demonstrate his presence.

Just as with Peter, God has approved you and has entrusted you with his plans. He trusts you and believes in you to carry them out and has sent his Spirit as a seal of his presence in you.

He also does not leave us alone in the doing. He has filled us with his Spirit to guide and work alongside us, co-laboring with us in what he has entrusted to us, living the gospel life.

All of us are entrusted with living out the gospel in our lives. However, each of us may have a different outpouring of the gospel work entrusted to us by God, with the salt and light of Christ shining through by living the Spirit-led gospel life while doctoring, mothering, cleaning, teaching, etc.

Many biblical figures were entrusted with work to do too and cooperated with God to bring it about. They labored to show the love of God to those around them. So you too labor together with the Spirit to do the work he has called you to do: grandmother, mother, sister, call center attendant, nurse, doctor, writer, teacher, janitor, yaya, architect, computer programmer. All of these may well be what and where God has called you, and he has trusted you to carry out his will and his gospel in these places.

Consider what God has entrusted to you and entrusted you with—all for his Kingdom advancement—and take courage to do it well with him. Knowing that he tests and approves of me and his Spirit dwells within me gives me the courage and enthusiasm to reach for the Spirit's hand and go forth to do his will. May his trust in you give you courage to carry out your role too.

Conclusion

Understanding who God is and what he can and cannot do builds a foundation of trust that grows confidence and encourages us to rest easily. Knowing that he is with us always, never leaves us, and always works for our good in and through all circumstances means that I have nothing to fear. There is no need for me to worry when God loves me so much that he already died that I may live.

A ship in the water is much easier to turn when the engine is on and the anchor is up. In other words, our working with the talents that we have been given is a much better place than being stuck in the mud and not doing anything. God will guide us even when we do not know what purpose something may have. When we are willing to trust in him for that talent. Once we get moving, the Spirit will engage with us to ensure that we are working for the well-being of God and others.

Whatever that gift or talent may be, bringing order through cleaning, increasing sales through advertising campaigns, showing love by toting children to softball practice—all of these show God's character working through you, shining his love and trust to the world. He is the God of order, of provision, of love, and more. And our talents reflect that into the world. He wants us to do well, and he actively works so that we in fact *do* and *are* well.

No matter the hard things and rough circumstances we walk through, God is with us and trusts us in our walk. Little by little we can build a meaningful mutual relationship, God and me, together. Relationships begin in a moment, but grow in intimacy, vulnerability, and trust over time. God is willing to put in the time and has already laid the perfect foundation in Christ Jesus. He loves us already, has sent his Spirit, and seeks our fellowship in others. He fights by our side. He has done all he can to create a two-way relationship with you. He just asks that you meet him there and open your heart, which he takes very, very good care of.

Discussion Guide

Deepen Your Understanding. Strengthen Your Trust. Grow in Faith.

Trusting God can be challenging, especially in difficult seasons. Our Trustworthy God: Discussion Guide is designed to help individuals and groups engage in meaningful conversations about God's faithfulness, His love, and His trust in us.

This companion guide provides thought-provoking questions, Scripture reflections, and practical applications to reinforce the core themes of Our Trustworthy God. Whether you're leading a small group, joining a Bible study, or reflecting on your own, this guide will help you:

- Explore biblical truths about God's trustworthiness

- Process doubts and challenges in a safe, faith-filled space

- Apply God's promises to your daily life

Discover the depth of God's love and faithfulness as you walk through this guide—because He is not only worthy of our trust, but He also delights in trusting us.

Download this guide FREE.

About the Author

A uthor and founder of InspiritEncourage, Sarah K. Howley writes Bible studies that reveal the transforming depth of Scripture and lead readers into a thriving relationship with God. Known for weaving Old and New Testament connections with warmth and insight, she invites believers to encounter God's truth in everyday life. She fuels her writing with espresso—and gratitude for any gluten-free/dairy-free dessert she didn't bake herself. Sarah and her husband support global initiatives for literacy and hunger relief.

You can find Sarah on Facebook and Instagram @inspiritencourage. To book Sarah as a speaker at your next event, please contact her through her website. For weekly encouragement and information on her latest releases, sign up for Sarah's newsletter at InspiritEncourage.com.

SARAH K. HOWLEY

InspiritEn-
courage

Also By Sarah K. Howley

Seeing the Old Testament in the Epistles
Ephesians: Experience God's Power
James: Know God's Wisdom
1&2 Thessalonians: Prepare for Christ's Return
Hebrews: Elevate Jesus
Philippians: Pursue Christ's Joy
1&2 Peter: Grow in Grace
Revelation: Worship the Lamb
Colossians & Philemon: Live Transformed
1,2&3 John: Dwell in Light
Romans: Trust the Faithful God

The Son Reveals the Father
I Am: An 8-Session Study of John
Heart: A 12-Session Study of Luke
Word: An 11-Session Study of Matthew
King: An 8-Session Study of Mark
Our Trustworthy God: How Much God loves You,
Joyfully Engages with You, and Trusts You

Women of the Old Testament Bible Studies
Hope: A Bible Study of Women in Jesus' Lineage

Faith (coming 2026)
Love (coming 2026)

Alive Again Bible Study on Forgiveness
Alive Again: Find Healing in in Forgiveness
Alive Again Bible Study: Find Healing in Forgive-
ness
Alive Again Forgiveness Prayer Journal

Endnotes

1. Wright, N.T. "Why We Have To Love Something to Know It." Aug 26, 2022. N.T. Wright Online, 5:04. https://youtu.be/S_68OD9kL Jo?si=fS5YSihzvZuAXQly

2. Thomas Jay Oord, *The Death of Omnipotence and the Birth of Amipotence* (SacraSage Press, 2023), 126.

3. Rachel Held Evans, *Inspired: Slaying Giants, Walking on Water, and Loving the Bible Again* (Nelson Books, 2018), xx.

4. "Strong's Greek: 1381. (Dokimazo)." BibleHub. https://biblehub.com/greek/1381.htm.

5. Though Moses may have killed to protect others, a seemingly "right" action, it was likely done through ungodly means. We do not have evidence that God approved of this killing.

6. Moses' father-in-law was a priest and likely instructed his household in the ways of God. Moses had been raised in an Egyptian home then ran away and lived in Midian. Midianites were descendants of Abraham through sons he had later in life (Genesis 25:1-4). Moses had spent time then in Midian with his father-in-law who was a priest of the area. We find later in Exodus 18 that he was likely a priest of Yahweh.

7. Schaser, Nicholas J. 2022. "Did God Harden Pharaoh's Heart?" Israel Bible Center. August 7, 2022. https://weekly.israelbiblecenter.com/did-god-harden-pharaohs-heart.

8. Additional References: *The God Who Trusts* by Curtis Holtzen. *God Is (Not) in Control* by Jason Clark. *The Death of Omnipotence and the Birth of Amipotence* by Thomas Jay Oord.

www.ingramcontent.com/pod-product-compliance
Lightning Source LLC
Chambersburg PA
CBHW071531120626
46550CB00006B/2418